Horses and Their Ancestors

HORSES

WHITTLESEY HOUSE

McGraw-Hill Book Company, Inc.

New York   Toronto   London

WILLIAM A. BURNS

Assistant to Director, American Museum of Natural History

Pictures by PAULA HUTCHISON

and their ancestors

A McGraw-Hill——American Museum of Natural History Publication

Also by William A. Burns with pictures by Paula Hutchison

A WORLD FULL OF HOMES

Published by Whittlesey House, a division of the McGraw-Hill Book Co.
Printed in the United States of America

Contents

The First Horses   6

Horses for Getting Places   13

Modern Horses and Their Relatives   19

Horses in War   26

Horses for Protection   28

Horses at Work   30

Horses and Jobs   36

Horses in the Making of Our Nation   39

Some Well-known Horses   43

Horses in Sport and in Fun   48

Horses in Story and in Art   54

the first horses

Many, many millions of years ago, there were no people on the earth at all. There were no cats. There were no dogs. There were no goats or cows or sheep.

And there were no horses.

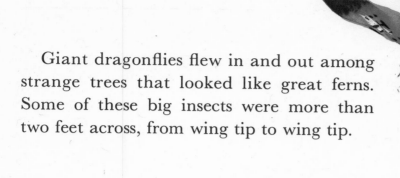

Giant dragonflies flew in and out among strange trees that looked like great ferns. Some of these big insects were more than two feet across, from wing tip to wing tip.

There were odd-looking reptiles, like the Dimetrodon (die-me-tro-don), that slept in the warm sun near the waters of marshy swamps.

Then there were flying reptiles, like the pterodactyls (ter-o-dak-tils). These looked like oversized, clumsy birds. They had claws on their wings, and they could not fly nearly so well as our birds of today.

But there were no horses of any kind on the face of the earth.

About sixty million years ago, there was a little animal that lived in both North America and Europe. We call it eohippus (ee-o-hip-us), from two Greek words that mean "dawn horse." It lived long before any people were on the earth. It was the first horse

Some of these little dawn horses were no larger than a fox. Some were about half the size of a Shetland pony. You would not think that eohippus looked much like a modern horse. It had four toes on each front foot, and each toe ended in a separate small hoof. It had only three toes on each hind foot, of which the middle toe was the largest.

Modern horses have teeth that can chew and grind hard grass. We do not think that eohippus could have eaten grass, because its teeth were different from those of the modern horse. Eohippus must have lived on tender, easy-to-chew buds and leaves. It could also have found soft seeds and small fruits to eat. An animal that lives on this kind of food is called a browser.

Little eohippus slowly became Equus (eek-wus), our modern horse. This change took millions of years. As scientists found new proof of this development, they gave new names to these later animals that were developing into Equus. Some of these animals are called Mesohippus (mes-o-hip-us), Merychippus (mer-ik-hip-us), and Pliohippus (ply-o-hip-us).

You remember that eohippus had four little hoofs on each of its front feet and three on its back feet. Equus, our modern horse, has one hoof on each foot. Its hoof is a hard, horny covering.

We do not know if eohippus had a mane or not. We know that its tail was longer, in proportion to its body, than that of a modern horse.

9

By the time that people appeared on the earth, the horse had changed from the small animal of earlier periods into Equus, or our modern horse. We might say that man and the horse grew up together.

When early man lived in caves, the horse roamed wild in great herds. People did not know then that they could catch and tame horses and put them to work. They thought of horses only as food to eat.

At this time there were many other wild animals that man knew. There were huge mammoths that looked something like our elephants but had long woolly coats to protect them from the cold. People hunted these mammoths for food and perhaps used some of the wool from their shaggy coats to keep themselves warm.

There were great sabertooth cats that hunted man and that man hunted. They were fierce beasts, with long curving fangs.

And there were cave bears. When people wanted a cave to live in, they drove the bears out so that they themselves could use the caves to keep their families sheltered from the cold and from other wild animals.

11

We know that the early people knew about horses and used them for food, because in some of their caves we have found piles of the bones of horses they ate. We have also found paintings on the cave walls. The artists of those days painted the story of their daily lives—of their hunting and of the animals they knew. By the time that people had learned how to paint, with colors made from earth and clay, they had also learned that horses could be tamed and made useful.

horses for getting places

Early man found out how to catch animals and raise them for food. He also found out that some animals could help him in his work. He tamed the dog, and it helped him in hunting. He tamed the wild cow and found he could get milk from it. He finally tamed the horse, at first, perhaps, in order to have a handy food supply nearby without hunting for it. But perhaps some boy or girl made friends with a young horse and kept it for a pet.

If you feed an animal and are kind to it and do not frighten it, you can usually get near enough to it to pet it. Cave children must have fed grass or leaves to their little horses. Sometimes they must have leaned their weight against their pet horses to show how much they loved to be near them. Slowly the young horses got used to being close to human beings.

One wonderful day, let us imagine, a boy or girl got the idea of climbing upon a pet horse's back. He or she may

have sat there a while. A young horse, unused to such things, would have trembled with fear! It might even have tried to throw its rider off. But at last it got used to the weight. It must have been a sight to see when cave children first proudly galloped their young horses past their mothers and fathers. And after a few people learned to ride, many people must have trained their horses to carry them.

We do not know how early people used horses, other than to ride them. In hunting, for example, they may have tied the body of a deer to their horse to be dragged home. They may have tied long poles to the horse, let them drag behind, and placed their burdens across the poles, as the Indians of the plains did. But since there are no painted or written records, we cannot be sure.

14

There were no carts or wagons or carriages. No one had invented the wheel yet. We see wheels in use so much today that we give little thought to them. But the wheel is one of man's great inventions, and it must have taken early man many thousands of years to find out how to make one. Our trains, automobiles, machinery, and even roller skates work by means of wheels.

We do not even know what the first wheels were like. Perhaps people hacked off a cross section of round tree trunk, bored a hole through the center, and stuck a pole through the hole. This would have made a rough kind of wheel and axle.

After the ax was invented, people could split logs into planks more easily. They may have made wheels out of some of these planks. There are carts today that roll on heavy wooden plank wheels.

Before writing was invented, people kept records by painting pictures or by carving in stone. In some of these old paintings and stone carvings we can see how people used horses, both for riding and for driving.

The ancient Assyrians carved beautiful pictures in stone. In one of these you can see spirited horses pulling light, fast chariots on a lion hunt.

We can see in Egyptian paintings that they used the horse both for riding and for pulling chariots.

The early Greeks knew about horses and loved to make wonderful lifelike sculptures of them.

From the first man who climbed up on a horse to the rider of today, people have found the horse a most useful animal. Before trains and airplanes, before automobiles and busses, horses were carrying people—bareback, in the saddle, or in carts, chariots, wagons, carriages, and sleighs.

When coaches were much more in use than they are today, there were public carriers as well as smaller private ones. Some of these coaches were very large, and it took four, six, or even eight horses to pull them. The early coaches had no springs, and a long trip must have been a dusty and tiring experience. No wonder that travelers looked forward to breaking their journeys at coaching inns. Here they could

rest and eat and drink while the horses were being changed.

In the fourteenth century, people traveled in huge coaches. The coach of this time had four great wheels, each with six heavy spokes. It was covered over with a roof that made it look like one of the covered wagons that crossed our American plains. It took six horses to pull it. The horses were not hitched in pairs, but singly, like sled dogs. The driver rode the horse nearest the coach. He had a long whip so that he could reach all the horses to make them go faster.

By the year 1690, springs had been invented, and riding was more comfortable. Now people could take a trip without being jarred and jounced like peas in a pod. The drivers could go faster. Some good drivers often made as much as sixty-five or seventy miles in twelve hours. Today, our powerful cars, on a safe road, cover that distance in an hour.

People sometimes say "cart" when they mean "wagon." A cart has only two wheels. A wagon has at least four. There are many kinds of carts. A cart still in use today is the Irish cart.

There are two types of Irish cart. The side cart is so made that four people can sit along the sides, facing out. This is very convenient and pleasant for looking at scenery as you roll along the road. The other type of Irish cart has double seats so that the people sit in pairs, back to back.

17

The people who live in Sicily make pretty little carts with huge wheels. These carts—wheels and all—are painted and decorated in gay colors. The horses or donkeys pulling the carts are also ornamented; bells, plumes, and bits of flashing mirror are fastened in their harness.

Gypsies in Hungary and Rumania traveled in wagons that also served them as homes. They lived in them much as some of us live in our trailers today. Like the Sicilian carts, the gypsy wagons were gaily painted.

The early Dutch pioneers in South Africa rode in high wagons when they traveled across the great continent. These trek wagons, as they were called, were sometimes pulled by horses. Sometimes, far from home, one of the great wheels would break and there would be no way of fixing it. Then the settlers had either to stay where they were or try to push ahead on foot.

The droshky is a light, four-wheeled open carriage, once very popular in Russia. Wealthy people kept their own droshkies, or they could hire one the way we rent a taxi today.

18

modern horses
and their relatives

We know that all the modern horses in the world began with little eohippus, which grew into the horse the cave man and other early people knew. Like all other animals, horses were affected by climate, differences in food, and interbreeding. We know by looking at them that all modern horses are not exactly alike. Let's look at some horses and relatives of the horse to see what makes them different from one another.

Out of the many kinds of horses that man tamed came a wonderful horse we call the Arabian. The Arabian always has a black skin but may have a coat of any color. We think that a pure white Arabian is one of the world's most beautiful horses. The Arabian has a broad forehead and a delicate muzzle with long, thin lips. Its neck is long and gracefully arched. It has a fine, flowing mane and tail. It is strong, tough, and swift and can live in dry desert country where food and water are scarce.

It is not unusual for an Arab who owns such a horse to think so much of it that he keeps both the mother horse and its foal, or young horse, in the same tent with his family. The horse in turn is said to protect its master like a watchdog.

The Arabian is an important horse in breeding history because its blood flows in some of the world's best horses. Whenever the Arabs went to war, they took their horses with them. Wherever they went, their horses crossed with other horses found in the invaded land. Much fine Arabian blood was thus mixed with that of local horses, improving the local breed. The Arabs went into North Africa and into Europe as far as Spain. In the other direction, they went as far as India.

The Spaniards had a fine horse they called a jineta and that we call a jennet. There are no pure-bred jennets today. It was a mixture of the horse that had developed in Europe and the Arabian. When the Spanish explorers sailed for America, they took some of their best horses with them. It must have been a hard trip for horses and men alike—all the way from Spain to the New World in slow ships.

In both North and South America, some of the Spaniards' horses escaped and became wild. They found the American plains and the pampas good places to live in. Because the ancestors of these wild horses came partly from Arabian stock, there is a chance that any Western cow pony has a little royal Arabian blood! Later on, we will find that the *real* wild horses in the Americas disappeared long before the Spaniards came here and that the New World was without horses until they were carried here in ships from Europe.

While the Arabs were raising fine light horses, the people of Europe were raising a larger, heavier horse. You remember how the knights of old looked. Their armor was so heavy that they could not climb up on their mounts without help. It took a big, strong horse to carry a knight with all his armor and weapons, especially when the horse itself wore armor at times. The Great Horse of the Middle Ages was purposely bred by horse raisers to carry knights. The Arabian horse would have been too light to be able to carry a man in armor for long.

The people of Europe also bred a lighter horse—the Celtic pony. It was small, only eleven to twelve hands high. (A "hand," in horse talk, is four inches—which is just about the width of a grownup's hand. A horse that is from eleven to twelve hands high is from

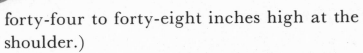

forty-four to forty-eight inches high at the shoulder.)

The Celtic pony, although small, was strong. One of its modern descendants is the Iceland pony.

The early Romans, when they invaded Britain, found that some fine horses were being raised there. Julius Caesar wrote in his soldier's diary of "fast chariots drawn by British horses." He thought so highly of these horses that he carried some back to Rome with him.

France had some fine horses, too. When a later conqueror, William, came to England from France in 1066, he had with him some horses from a part of France called Normandy. Many of these Norman horses were crossed with the English horses.

You remember that the horses that we call "wild horses" in the Americas were really tame horses that learned to live by themselves after escaping from their owners. The only really wild horse that might be left in the world today is a horse that has the long and hard-to-say name of a Russian explorer.

22

It is Przewalski's (pruz-val-ski's) horse. It is found in western Mongolia and is a rather small horse with a short mane and a reddish coat.

The horse has many relatives in its large family. One of its closest relatives is the onager (on-a-jer), sometimes called the kiang (key-ang). It is also called the Asiatic wild ass, although it is not an ass at all. It is about twelve hands high and has a reddish coat, with a dark stripe down its back. It has a tail like a donkey's, with a dark tuft at the end. There are not many onagers left. Explorers tell us that they are animals with a great deal of curiosity and will come into camp to find out what is going on. But they are swift and are not easily caught.

The familiar striped zebra is an African member of the horse family. Zebras have been tamed, and there are written records that tell of their being used to pull chariots in Roman parades.

Not much more than eighty years ago, there were still quaggas (kwah-gahs) in Africa. When the Dutch settled in South

Africa in the early nineteenth century, they found an animal that was striped on its front half and almost unstriped on its back half. It looked something like a zebra in front and a horse in back. But the settlers hunted the quagga and now there are none left. The stripes of the quagga, like those of the zebra, helped it to hide from its natural enemies. But it could not hide from the settler's rifle.

Our own pretty little donkeys are descended from the wild asses of northern Africa. Like the other wild relatives of the horse, they have a dark stripe down the back. Unlike the neigh of a horse, a donkey's bray is loud enough to hurt your ears. Donkeys need less food than horses do. Many people keep them as work animals when they cannot get or cannot afford a horse. There are working donkeys in almost every part of the world, particularly in Africa, Spain, Italy, Mexico, and in the southwestern part of our own United States.

Now that we have met the donkey, we ought to talk a little bit about mules. A mule has a donkey for a father and a horse for a mother. Mules are very strong, sure-footed animals. Many farmers prefer them to horses for farm work. The Army has used many mules as pack animals and for pulling loads. Mules have also been widely used by prospectors because their sure-footedness makes them better for riding, and carrying loads, along dangerous trails.

A hinny has a horse for a father and a donkey for a mother. It is not thought highly of as a working animal, and so we do not hear much about hinnies.

There are two living animals that you would never think were related to the horse. One is the tapir and the other is the rhinoceros. Tapirs have four toes on each front foot and three on each back foot, the same arrangement as little eohippus had.

The rhinoceros is another relative of the horse. Once it lived in North America and Europe, but now we find it only in India, Java, Sumatra, and Africa.

25

horses in war

More than five thousand years ago, men found out that they could use horses in warfare. The Assyrians, the ancient Egyptians, the Romans, and many others used the horse-drawn chariot in battle. Some chariots had sharp knives fastened to the hubs of the wheels.

Foot soldiers were almost helpless against chariots. But when soldiers rode on horseback they could usually beat men in chariots. Mounted men could ride swiftly up to the enemy, strike hard, turn in a moment, and gallop away—all before a chariot could get ready.

Some of the world's most famous fighters were horsemen. In the eleventh century the Mongol ruler Genghis Khan led his mounted warriors in battle and almost won what was then the known world. His troops were such masters at fighting on horseback that even modern generals study and learn from the way they planned an attack.

The knights of old fought with long lances, clubs, axes, and swords. But when guns were

26

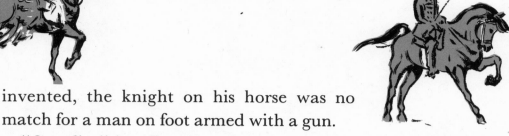

invented, the knight on his horse was no match for a man on foot armed with a gun.

"Cavalier" is a French word meaning "horseman." One of its modern meanings is "gentleman," because in the old days, only gentlemen rode horseback. The first cavaliers were mounted swordsmen.

The Arab rode his prized horse into battle. When these desert fighters defended their land against enemies, they often rode in a body, shooting their long-barreled rifles as they galloped. It must have been a wild sight to see them, their robes flying in the wind, plunging their beautiful horses down a steep sand dune without fear.

Horses played an important part in the American Revolution. George Washington's horse was supposed to have been half Arabian. We have all read that Paul Revere rode a horse to warn the colonists that the British were coming.

In the war between the North and the South, horses were needed for mounted troops and to pull guns and supplies.

horses for protection

It is only a step from using horses in war to using them for patrol and peace duties.

In Canada there are thousands of miles of thinly settled country. The roads connecting one settlement with another are few. The Royal Canadian Mounted Police have a tremendous area to cover in their work, and automobiles are of little use when it is a question of going into bush country.

The Mounties cover much of their territory on horseback. Carrying a small quantity of food, the mounted policemen ride by day and sleep by night. They live off the country as they go. A mounted policeman may be gone a long time, but thanks to his horse he gets out of the woods and back to headquarters safely.

The automobile still cannot replace the horse in some city police work, for example, in controlling heavy traffic. The mounted policeman can see over a tangle of trucks and passenger cars and can thread his way quickly through the traffic jam to straighten it out.

At parades, mounted policemen can keep crowds in better order than can men in automobiles or on motorcycles. Troublesome groups seem to be more easily managed by police on horseback than by police in cars. Mounted men in parks can cover more ground than men on foot or in motorcars. They can also get to places that police cars cannot reach.

The police horse must be a special trained horse. It must be of a certain size (in some cities, of a particular color), and between four and seven years of age. Its training often takes from two to three years. In the police academy, where the horses are schooled, each horse learns to go through heavy traffic without fear, to stand still and wait when its rider has to leave it for a time, and to obey all the commands of the policeman.

After the police horse has served in the department until it is old, it is retired and lives in comfort for the rest of its life on a horse farm. Police horses are never sold to work as delivery horses after retirement.

horses at work

Before steam, gasoline, and electric power, horses did most of the world's work. Even though many things are done by machine nowadays, horses are still important in getting man's work accomplished.

Less than ten years ago, there were over seven million horses working on farms in the United States. The farmer's horse, like the farmer himself, must do a little bit of everything. In the spring the horse may pull a plow. In the summer it may pull a hay wagon. At harvest time it may pull the reaper. In the winter it may pull a sleigh to take the farmer and his family to town or to church.

On large farms, especially in our Middle West, machines do the work of horses in a much shorter time. But on small farms, the horse is still a valuable work animal.

In the Near East—in Syria, Lebanon, and Jordan—horses are used today to grind wheat or corn if there is no other power at hand. The horse pushes against a long pole that is attached to the upper millstone. As the horse moves around in a big circle, the stone goes round and round, grinding the grains into flour or meal against the lower millstone. Old horses do such work better than young horses because they are less skittish.

Fifty years ago, before electric power was common, people went from one part of town to another in horsecars. Pulling these was hard work, especially when cars were crowded and hills were steep. In some hilly towns there was a special platform on the back of the horsecars. On the trip downhill, the horse rode on the platform. In winter, the horses wore warm blankets. In summer, horses often wore big straw hats, with holes to allow their ears to stick out.

Owners of small mines still use horses to haul the broken coal out of the mine. A mine horse must not be too many hands high. A small, but strong, horse is better fitted to pull loads of coal through low, narrow tunnels than is a big horse. In the Southwest, small donkeys, called burros, are also used to work in mines.

The lumberman's horse has hard work to do. But at least its work is out in the sunshine and fresh air. The big work horse in the lumber camp must "snake" out the logs and then pull the log sled to a shipping point. The foreman or owner may ride a fine saddle horse from job to job.

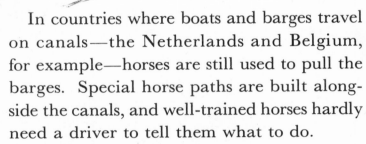

In countries where boats and barges travel on canals—the Netherlands and Belgium, for example—horses are still used to pull the barges. Special horse paths are built alongside the canals, and well-trained horses hardly need a driver to tell them what to do.

Some horses work for fishermen. They pull the high wagons loaded with nets down to the sea. They help the fishermen haul in the nets if they are fishing on the beach. When fishing is bad, the fishermen sometimes gather loads of seaweed for sale and the horses pull the seaweed back to town.

It was not very many years ago that horses were pulling fire engines to fires. When the alarm sounded, the firemen would slide down the brass poles, hitch up their horses in seconds, and tear out of the firehouse with smoke and sparks streaming from their red and gold engines. Often a spotted fire dog, a Dalmatian, ran beside the engine. Today there are few, if any, fire horses left in the United States. But firemen still keep Dalmatians in their firehouses.

The junkman who sells secondhand things or buys old bottles, rags, and newspapers is a familiar sight. His wagon usually has a string of cowbells tied across two posts, so that housewives who want to sell their junk can hear him coming. Many boys and girls make pin money by saving newspapers and bottles for the junkman.

Everyone knows the milkman's horse. Even in this day of automobiles there are

many horse-drawn milk wagons with big rubber tires. A good milkman's horse will move up to the next house while the milkman is delivering milk to the one before. In some parts of the country, if you are up very early, you may hear the milkman's horse clip-clopping home after a night's work.

A gay spot of color in the Netherlands is the vegetable man's wagon. Even in the large cities you can find long, flat wagons with low sides, piled high with tomatoes, carrots, beets, eggplants, and potatoes. There are also some not so familiar things—heaps of an orange mushroom called cantarella, little bananas from Java, and strange fruits from the East Indies.

In our own land, an early messenger of spring is the flower man with his horse and wagon. He drives slowly up the street, selling flowers and plants. You can buy red geraniums or trailing ivy for your window or —if you have space to set them out—a box of pansies.

One kind of horse and wagon that has almost disappeared is the knife and scissors grinder's. He has a fine red wagon, roofed over to keep out sun and rain. Big windows in the sides let the children see him at work, sharpening big butcher knives and scissors. It is a fine sight to see the golden shower of sparks from his busy wheel.

Far from city streets, the prospector's pack horses carry his food and tools, enough to last for months while he looks for precious metals. The prospector rides the lead horse; the other horses carry bacon, tea, flour, dried fruit, sugar, and other things the prospector will need. Packing a horse or a mule is not as easy as it looks. You must know the various hitches or knots in order to tie the load on so that it will not slip. You must know how to put heavy objects in the right place. The load must be well balanced and not be too heavy for the horse.

horses and jobs

Its many uses have made the horse very valuable to man. In keeping horses and in using them, many thousands of people have found work.

Building beautiful carriages for people to ride in was once a craft in which many men made their living. Some of our modern automobile-body makers began by making carriage bodies. Somebody had to drive the horses. Coachmen had to be well-trained and skillful drivers. They sat up on their high boxes and handled their horses in all kinds of weather.

Teamsters drove heavy wagons in the cities, carrying freight between the railroads and ships and the warehouses. They were proud of their big, powerful horses and of their expert driving.

Generations of innkeepers owed their bread and butter to horsemen and to travelers who went by coach. The inns they stayed at were the first hotels.

36

Many a boy, in those days, learned to make fine harness for his living. First he had to spend a long time learning from an expert harness worker.

Saddle makers are still busy men. They make fine Western saddles for cowboys and fine English saddles for riders in the park.

You can still find blacksmith shops in some of our towns. Horses must wear shoes of iron, and from time to time these need repairing or replacing.

People who ride need special clothes. Bootmakers make riding boots from rich, glowing leathers for cowboys and for people who ride for pleasure and for sport.

Tailors design riding costumes for riding and for hunting. Special hats are worn for riding. But the cowboy prefers the blue jeans he calls levis and his Western hat.

It was not always possible for city people to keep a horse and carriage. Thousands of people found work in renting horses and carriages to other people. You can still hire a horse or a carriage to ride in the park.

37

Hay and feed stores still sell corn, hay, oats, bran, and other foods to people for their horses.

Jockeys make their living riding horses. Stable boys take care of horses.

Many girls and boys want to be animal doctors, or veterinarians, when they grow up. Then they can treat sick horses and other animals.

The covers of baseballs are made of horse-hide. So are the finest baseball gloves.

Some of the best mattresses are made of horsehair.

Violin bows are made of long white hairs from horses' tails.

Farmers use much bone meal as fertilizer in their fields.

To keep us well, doctors give us "shots" of protective substances, sometimes made from horse's blood.

38

horses in the making of our nation

There were no horses on the American continent when the Spanish explorers brought sixteen of them from Havana, Cuba, in 1519. Seventeen actually arrived in North America because a young horse was born on the way. What had happened to all the horses, eohippus and the others? There was once a land bridge—a strip of land—that reached from North America to Asia. You can still see where this connecting land was by looking at the map below. The dotted lines show where the land was before it sank under the water. The horses in America, in their wanderings, found this strip of land and many of them traveled, by slow stages, into Asia and then into Europe. Some of them wandered southward down the length of North America and found another strip of land—the Isthmus of Panama. Crossing over this land bridge, they spread out through South America. The Isthmus of Panama is still there. You can see it on this map.

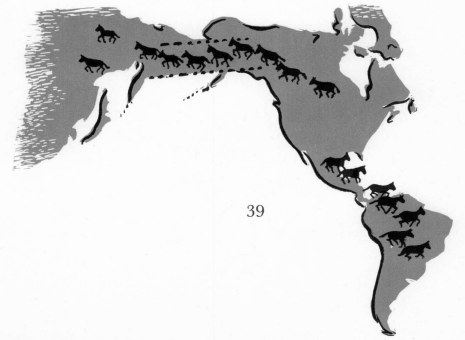

39

At last, all the horses that stayed in North and South America died out. We can only guess why they became extinct. There were no meat-eating animals that could have eaten all the horses. There was plenty of good grass in both North and South America. Perhaps it was some sickness that killed them off; we really do not know. After the early horses disappeared, there were no more horses in the Americas until the Spaniards brought the modern horse from Europe.

The horses that the Spaniards brought here have helped America to grow into a strong nation. Let's see what part horses have played in the growth of our nation.

The early Spaniards used their horses to explore the New World. They found good places to build cities. They discovered wide rivers and pleasant valleys. Word of their discoveries reached the other countries of Europe, and people wanted to come to the new land to live.

The early colonists depended upon the horses they brought with them from Europe to do the heavy work of hauling lumber for their homes. They also needed horses to keep in touch with the growing towns and cities in the New World. Mail was carried on horseback and by coach.

The first pioneers found out about the West by exploring the new land. Horses made this exploring possible.

When the pioneers came back to tell of the great land in the West, whole families—even whole villages—went West. They sometimes traveled in Conestoga wagons, the covered wagon of the American plains. Riders on horseback protected these long lines of "prairie schooners" from attack by unfriendly Indians.

As people found places where they wanted to live, they settled. Villages grew into towns and towns into cities. Before the pony express, in 1860, mail between the East and California had to go by ship, wagon train, and stagecoach. Pony-express riders galloped the mail from St. Joseph, Missouri, to Sacramento, California—nearly two thousand miles in eight days. Horses were changed about every ten miles for the whole distance.

41

As the West opened up and the settlers discovered how rich the land was, they found that they needed more and more horses. Some were used for farm work. Many were used by cowboys who looked after the great herds of cattle that fed on the grasses of the plains. There was nothing more important to a cowboy than his horse, and he took good care of it at all times.

Before the railroads were built across the country, the wagon trains carried freight and the stagecoaches carried passengers. It took many weeks of hard driving to cross the country from coast to coast. When the trail was cut by a river, the people built big rafts to float their wagons and coaches to the other side.

After the railroads were built, wagon trains and stage-coaches were used only for travel between areas not served by the railroad lines. When the automobile was introduced, the stagecoach disappeared except in stories of the Old West. But without the horse, the West might have remained an un-settled region for a long time.

some well-known horses

Today there are many fine horses, all bred from the first true modern horse, Equus. People have found out that they can breed the kind of horse they need for a particular job by careful selection. Some horses are suited for heavy work, some for racing, some for playing games like polo, some for children to ride. Experts on horses tell us that there are some sixty recognized breeds of horses in the world today. Some of the breeds that we might come across—on a farm, pulling a heavy wagon, racing, taking vacationists for a ride, or walking in a zoo or park with small boys on their backs—are shown below.

The Thoroughbred was first bred in England. It is a mixture of English racing and Arabian stock. All racing horses at recognized meets must be registered Thoroughbreds. The name Thoroughbred applies only to the one breed of horse with that name. Sometimes people say "Thoroughbred" when they mean any animal with carefully chosen ancestors.

43

The Morgan is a fine horse that originated in Vermont. It used to be a good harness horse but is now raised for riding.

The Hackney was imported from England. It was a spirited high-stepping horse and used to put on a fine show when pulling the family carriage.

The Standard-bred horse resembles the Thoroughbred but is somewhat smaller. It is the horse that pulls a light racing sulky in the trotting races.

The Quarter Horse is particularly popular in the Southwestern part of the United States. It is a favorite of cowpunchers because of its ease of handling and its speed.

The American Saddle Horse is a horse you might see at a horse show. It is easy to train and puts on a fine show.

The Tennessee Walking Horse is another American-bred horse. It traces its beginnings to one Kentucky horse named Allan, who was taken to Tennessee as a young horse. Walking Horses make fine horses for pleasure riding.

The name palomino indicates a color rather than a breed. A palomino horse is a lovely golden color with silvery mane and tail.

The smallest of our horses is the Shetland pony. It came from the Shetland Islands, north of Scotland. It is sometimes only nine hands high, or about as high as your mother's yardstick. Recently breeders have produced a pony not larger than a good-sized dog.

45

Among work horses, the dapple-gray Percheron is one of the favorites. It is descended from the Great Horse of the Middle Ages. Its ancestors carried knights in armor. The Percheron, weighing over two thousand pounds, is now used for heavy work of other sorts.

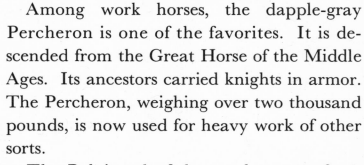

The Belgian draft horse also came from the Great Horse. It is much like the Percheron but its color is usually chestnut.

The largest of the work horses is the Shire, a descendant of the English Great Horse. It sometimes weighs over twenty-two hundred pounds (two hundred pounds more than a ton!). It often stands seventeen hands high and has thick bunches of hair or "feathers" on its legs.

46

The fine horses that the Spaniards brought to the New World were bred, and the missions, traders, and Indians got some of the young horses. When they escaped from their owners they became "wild." Such horses are now called mustangs. There are few pure-blooded mustangs today.

The strong, wiry little pony of the Indians is called a cayuse.

A polo pony is not a special breed. Any good small horse that is trained to play polo is called a polo pony.

There are many other fine horses—too many to tell about here. By this time you can see what an effect man has had on horses. Let's see what effect horses have had on man and his fun.

horses in sport and in fun

All through history, the horse has been man's companion in the hunt. Fox hunting is a popular sport in England and in some parts of our own country. Horses and hounds join in the chase. "Hunters," as the horses are called, have to be good jumpers. When the fox goes under the hedge or fence or over a stone wall, the hunter must go over to follow it.

Wild boars are very dangerous animals. In Europe and in Asia, people hunt boars on horseback.

An early form of hunting on horseback was done with the aid of trained birds called falcons. The falcon was taught to ride hooded on the wrist of the hunter until game was seen. Then the hood was taken off the bird's head and it flew after its prey. When the falcon had downed its quarry, it returned to its master's wrist and was hooded again until the next try.

Another way of hunting from horseback is with the bola. The bola is made up of two or three stone balls fastened to strong cords. It is swung around the head and then let go at the prey. If it strikes, the whirling stones twist the cords around the animal, throwing it until the rider can reach it. The bola is used in South America for some of the same purposes as we use the lasso.

Horse racing is a very old sport. Almost three thousand years ago, horses were raced at the Olympic games. The Greeks raced chariots and also horses ridden by young boys. As far back as 508 B.C., a young jockey fell off his horse. The horse kept on running and came in first. The story goes that the riderless horse got the prize for finishing the race alone.

Modern horse racing is colorful. The beautiful horses, the gay silks of the jockeys, and the excitement of the race itself makes this sport a popular pastime.

Polo is an exciting and sometimes dangerous game. It was played in Persia and in India hundreds of years ago. Modern polo arose in the nineteenth century when British cavalry officers stationed in India watched the original game and decided it would be fun to play. The idea of polo is to hit the ball past the opponents' goal post with a mallet.

One of the most exciting and dangerous forms of horse racing is the steeplechase. It is really a cross-country race on horseback. The rider must jump over fences, hurdles, wide ditches, water jumps, and brush-piled obstacles, and win over a big field of rivals.

The squires of the days of knighthood were boys who were studying to become knights. One of their favorite games, and most useful as training, was tilting at a target. The tilting squire carried a short, blunt wooden spear. He galloped

50

his horse toward a target fastened to a beam on a post. At
the other end of the target was a sack, usually wet or filled
with flour. When he hit the target, the other end of the
beam swung around quickly and he had to duck in time or
the sack would hit him on the back of his head.

Another old game that is still played on
horseback is Japanese mounted archery.
Long ago, Japanese knights made a game of
galloping past targets, shooting arrows as they
went by. It gave them practice for war when
they might have to shoot from the saddle.

Horses play a part in bullfighting. They
are ridden during part of the fight. We do
not permit bullfighting in our country because we think it is too cruel for both horse
and bull.

Just plain horseback riding is a popular
sport all over the world. In the city parks
and on shady country roads you see people
enjoying a ride. It is not as easy as it looks.
You must learn how to mount, how to sit,

51

and how to handle your horse. You must remember, too, that a horse is not a machine and needs gentle handling.

People like to watch horses in action. Some horses are highly trained to perform in the theater and at the circus. They seem to be able to count or to spell out letters. You and I know that the horse cannot really spell or add but is following cues or instructions given by its trainer.

Rodeos are thrilling to watch. In the rodeo, cowboys try to ride horses that may still be half wild. It takes a great deal of skill to stay on the back of a bucking bronco.

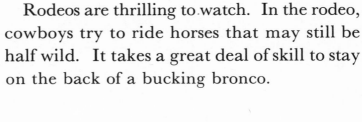

The horse show offers many attractions. A favorite is the horse that jumps, with its rider, through a paper hoop.

52

Ponies share in the children's fun. The pony walk is a familiar sight at the zoo.

We have all seen children on the back of a friendly little pony in the street, having their pictures taken.

The rocking horse is a popular toy with children. And at the amusement park you can find the whole family going round and round, up and down, on the merry-go-round.

In the movies and on the TV screen we often see exciting horse pictures, most of them about the Old West.

horses in story and art

People have loved horses so much that they have made up wonderful stories about them. Thousands of years ago, they told tales of magic horses, horses with wings, horses with horns, and even horses that talked.

Perhaps when people first noticed the sea horse they thought that the pretty little creature was a tiny horse that lived in the ocean. We know that the sea horse is really a fish.

The ancients thought that Neptune, the god of the sea, rode in a chariot pulled by great sea horses.

Not too long ago people still believed in the unicorn, whose name means "one horn." They thought it was a splendid horse with a long ivory horn growing out of the center of its forehead. We can still see the unicorn— on old shields and tapestries.

The Greeks believed that there were creatures who were half man, half horse. They called them centaurs. Some centaurs were very wise and could teach human beings much that they should know.

54

The Greeks also thought that the sun god, Apollo, drove the fiery horses of the sun across the sky every day. They told a story of how Apollo's son, when he was granted his wish to drive his father's horses, was killed because he was not strong enough to control them.

Another Greek story tells of Pegasus, a beautiful horse with wings. No one had ever ridden him until a youth named Bellerophon put a golden bridle over his head and became his master.

You have heard of the famous Trojan horse, the wooden horse of Troy. The hero, Ulysses, had a great hollow wooden horse built outside the gates of the city of Troy, and he hid in it with his men. The people of Troy were told that it was a gift offering and broke down part of the city wall to drag it inside. During the night Ulysses and his men got out of the horse, opened the city gates, and let in the rest of the Greek army. Troy was beaten by a hollow wooden horse.

55

Like the people of early times, our modern writers have written wonderful stories about horses.

In *The Legend of Sleepy Hollow,* by Washington Irving, a Headless Horseman chased poor Ichabod Crane and stole his sweetheart.

Gulliver's Travels, by Jonathan Swift, tells of a land where horses rule over man. These horses were called by the made-up name of Houyhnhnms because Swift thought the name sounded like a whinny.

Bookstore shelves are crowded with amusing and stirring stories in which the hero is a horse. Horse stories are as popular today as they ever were.

Many pieces of music take horses into account too. The famous old song "Do Ye Ken John Peel?" sings of John Peel's hounds and his horses.

"The Ride of the Valkyries," the opening of the third act of a famous opera by the composer Wagner, tells in music of the wild galloping of the horses ridden by maidens from the Norse heaven, Valhalla.

Ferde Grofé, in his *Grand Canyon Suite,* lets you listen to the clip-clop of the donkeys' feet as they wind along the trail. If you listen closely, you can hear them bray, too.

People have been painting horses ever since the days, many thousands of years ago, when man was still living in caves, and they have been painting, drawing, sculpturing, weaving, and using horses in decoration ever since. The ancient Persians often drew beautiful horses in their hand-written books.

Chinese artists made lovely blue horses in porcelain.

People even put horse designs on plates.

Tapestries or woven wall fabrics were needed in years gone by to cover the cold stone walls in castles and palaces. Many wonderful tapestries show horses in war and hunting scenes.

In the game of chess, the knight is shown as a horse's head. Many chess sets are finely carved in ivory, jade, gold and silver, and fine woods.

In the modern weaving of Sweden we find lively horses.

And in the design of our own Pennsylvania Dutch.

And in Dutch pottery mugs like this one.

59

And tiles. And in silver work. And on inn signs.

And on the farmer's weather vane that points the direction of the wind over the barn.

Horses have affected the games we play, the art we enjoy, the music we listen to, and even our daily speech. Here are some "horsy" expressions you hear every day.

"To set the cart before the horse." To do something backward.

"A dark horse!" An unknown candidate who comes up from behind and wins.

"Don't look a gift horse in the mouth." Don't find fault with something you got for nothing.

"A horse of another color." A different thing entirely.

"You can lead a horse to water but you cannot make it drink." You cannot make people do what they do not want to do.

"To swap horses in midstream." To change the way you are doing a thing right in the middle of the job.

There are many more, of course. And there are horsy expressions that apply to people too. We all know people who are "as skittish as colts." We may know people, too, who are "as stubborn as a mule." We all hope that we ourselves show "horse sense."

It is plain that horses are on our minds more than we realize. We have seen the work they have done for us. We know how they have affected the history of the world. We have seen the part they played in the opening of our own great West. We write about them, paint them, make statues of them, sing about them, and put them into our daily speech. One thing is plain—that the horse *must* be one of our favorite animals.

index

America, first horses in, 20–21, 39–40
American Saddle Horse, 45
Apollo, 55
Arabian horses, 19–20, 27
Archery, 51
Art, horses in, 12, 16, 58–60
Assyrians, 16, 26

Barge horse, 32
Baseball, 38
Belgian horse, 46
Bellerophon, 55
Blacksmith, 37
Bola, 49
Boots, 37
Breeds of horses, 43–47
Bullfighting, 51
Burro, 31

Caesar, Julius, 22
Carriages, 36, 37
Carts, 17–18
Cavalier, 27
Cave bear, 11
Cave men, horses tamed by, 13–14
Cave paintings, 12
Cayuse, 47
Celtic pony, 21–22

Centaur, 54
Chariots, 16, 22, 26, 49
Chess, 59
Circus, 52
Coaches, 16–17, 36, 42
Coachman, 36
Conestoga wagon, 41
Cow pony, 21, 47
Cowboys, 37, 42, 52

"Dawn horse" (eohippus), 8–9, 19
Dimetrodon, 7
Donkey, 18, 24
Droshky, 18

Egyptians, 16, 26
Eohippus, 8–9, 19
Equus, 9, 10, 43

Falcon, 48
Farm horse, 30
Fire engine, 33
Fisherman's horse, 32
Flower wagon, 34

Genghis Khan, 26
Great Horse, 21, 46
Greeks, ancient, 16, 49, 54–55
Grofé, Ferde, 57
Gypsy wagon, 18

Hackney, 44
"Hand," 21
Harness, 37
Headless Horseman, 56
Hinny, 25
Horse show, 52
Horsecars, 31
"Horsy" sayings, 60–61
Houyhnhms, 56
Hunter, 48
Hunting, 48–49

Iceland pony, 22
Indians, 14, 47
Innkeeper, 36
Inns, 16, 36
Irish cart, 17
Irving, Washington, 56

Jennet, 20
Jockey, 38
Junkman's horse, 33

Kiang, 23
Knights, 21, 26, 50

Land bridge, 39
Lumber horse, 32

Mammoth, 11
Merychippus, 9

Mesohippus, 9
Middle Ages, 21, 22
Milkman's horse, 33–34
Mill horse, 30
Mine horse, 31
Morgan, 44
Mule, 24–25
Music, horses in, 57
Mustang, 47
Myths, 54–55

Norman horses, 22

Onager, 23

Palomino, 45
Pegasus, 55
Percheron, 46
Pictures of horses, 12, 16, 58–60
Pioneers, 40–41
Pliohippus, 9
Police horse, 28–29
Polo, 50
Polo pony, 47
Ponies, 53
    Celtic, 21–22
    Iceland, 22
    polo, 47
    Shetland, 45
    western, 21, 47

Pony express, 41
Prairie schooner, 41
Prospector's horse, 35
Proverbs, horses in, 60–61
Przewalski's horse, 22–23
Pterodactyl, 7

Quagga, 23–24
Quarter Horse, 44

Racing, 49, 50
Revere, Paul, 27
Rhinoceros, 25
Riding, 14, 51
Riding costumes, 37
Rodeo, 52
Romans, 22, 26
Royal Canadian Mounted Police, 28

Sabertooth cat, 11
Saddle, 37
Sayings, horses in, 60–61
Scissors grinder, 35
Sea horse, 54
Serum, 38
Shetland pony, 45
Shire horse, 46
Sicilian cart, 18
Side cart, 17
Spanish explorers, 20, 39–40
Springs, 17
Stagecoach, 41, 42

Standard-bred horse, 44
Steeplechase, 50
Stories of horses, 54–56
Swift, Jonathan, 56

Tapir, 25
Teamster, 36
Tennessee Walking Horse, 45
Thoroughbred horse, 43
Tilting, 50–51
Trek wagon, 18
Trojan horse, 55

Ulysses, 55
Unicorn, 54

Vegetable wagon, 34
Veterinarian, 38
Violin bow, 38

Wagner, Richard, 57
Wagon train, 41, 42
Wagons, 16, 17, 36, 41
War horses, 21, 22, 26–27
Washington, George, 27
Western horses, 20–21, 42, 47
Wheel, invention of, 15
Wild ass, 23, 24
Wild horses, 20–23
William the Conqueror, 22

Zebra, 23